YOUR KNOWLEDGE HAS VALUE

- We will publish your bachelor's and
  master's thesis, essays and papers

- Your own eBook and book -
  sold worldwide in all relevant shops

- Earn money with each sale

Upload your text at www.GRIN.com
and publish for free

Bibliographic information published by the German National Library:

The German National Library lists this publication in the National Bibliography; detailed bibliographic data are available on the Internet at http://dnb.dnb.de .

Imprint:

Copyright © 2019 GRIN Verlag
Print and binding: Books on Demand GmbH, Norderstedt Germany
ISBN: 9783668959491

This book at GRIN:

https://www.grin.com/document/490494

G. Nzowa

Human Resource Mangement in Education

GRIN Verlag

GRIN - Your knowledge has value

Since its foundation in 1998, GRIN has specialized in publishing academic texts by students, college teachers and other academics as e-book and printed book. The website www.grin.com is an ideal platform for presenting term papers, final papers, scientific essays, dissertations and specialist books.

Visit us on the internet:

http://www.grin.com/

http://www.facebook.com/grincom

http://www.twitter.com/grin_com

HUMAN RESOURCE MANAGEMENT IN EDUCATION

QUESTIONS AND ANSWERS

QUESTION ONE: Find out about five basic characteristics you want to be possessed by the employees in your ideal organization, then suggest the methods to be used to obtain people with those qualities.

QUESTION TWO: Explain the evolution in understanding treatment and use of people who are working in an organization. Identify the key concepts used to refer to those people and their management at different times in the evolution process.

QUESTION THREE: Discuss the major issues related to the government employees' management in schools in Tanzania.

QUESTION ONE

According to Aswathappa, (2009), the term Organization refers to a group of people working together to achieve a set of goals, those people who work in the organization have structure patterns of interactions, meaning that they expect each other to complete certain tasks in an organized way. Rafael, (1996), defined an Organization as structured social system consisting of groups and individuals working together to meet some agreed objectives.

Heathfield, (2018), in the other hand defined an employee as an individual who was hired by an employer to do a specific job. The employee is hired by the employer after an application and interview process results in his or her selection as an employee. This selection occurs after the applicant is found by the employer to be the most qualified applicant to do the job. Therefore, for an Organization to be successful in achieving its desirable goals and objectives, it requires quality employees.

Due to the fact that employees are the most important assets in the organization, in my ideal Organization I would like to have employees with the following characteristics as explained below;

First, strong work ethic – despite the fact that an employee need to have all the necessary knowledge, skills, attitude and aptitude, but when employees possess strong work ethics, the Organization's maintenance cost decreases because employees will be well aware of their duties and responsibilities towards the Organization. Reddy, (2015) argues, employees with strong work ethics will realize that they should not do any damage to any of the machines and equipment are given to them as they are very valuable for the Organization and doing damage to these things will be a wrong act, so automatically things will be taken care of and everything will work systematically. Therefore, employees with strong work ethics will do the following to the Organization;

- Increase in productivity
- Employees will work in team
- There will be no trouble in the working environment
- Will create good image of the Organization to the public
- Employees will be able to make ethical decisions
- Legal issue will decrease in the Organization. Gupta, (2011) postulates that, employees with strong work ethics are able to settle all grievances and disputes by mutual negotiations, conciliation and voluntary arbitration.

Second, self-motivated employees who can work effectively with little direction is another basic characteristic for employees. Aswathappa, (2009) argues that, motivation among employees is reflected in a passion to work for reasons that goes beyond money or status and they are quality oriented. Self-motivation among the employees is a primary means of realizing the Organizational goals. Employees who are self-motivated will lead to;

- Improve the overall efficiency of the Organization
- Build friendly relationship among employees hence creating the co-operative work environment
- Achieve employees' personal goals
- Employees job satisfaction
- Self-development of employees.

Hanson, (2003) in the other hand stipulates some qualities a self-motivated employee possesses including;

- Intensity of will (determination)
- Commitment (belief in goal)
- Self confidence

Therefore, for an Organization to be successful and competitive, employees should be highly self-motivated.

Third, team-oriented - many Organizations succeed based on the work of teams and entire departments, not just individuals. According to Mustafa, Glavee-Geo & Rice (2017), the self-managing teams do better than when they are supervised from the above. When the team has new ideas they can sit together to brainstorm ideas hence creating create more effective solutions to their Organization's problems. Working together for a human is a more productive process than working in isolation. Teamwork also maximizes the chances of learning from each other experiences. Team members can also gain from each other. Every individual is different and has some qualities. One can always benefit something or the other from his team members which would help him in the long run (Wehbe, 2017).

Tasks are accomplished at a faster pace when it is done by a team rather than an individual. An individual will definitely take more time to perform if he is single handedly responsible for everything. Wehbe, (2017), postulates that, when employees work together, they start helping each other and responsibilities are shared and thus it reduces the work load and work pressure. Every team member is assigned one or the other responsibility according to his specialization, level of interest and thus the output is much more efficient and faster (Williams, Duray, & Reddy, (2006).

> "*Coming together is a beginning. Keeping together is progress. Working together is success*" - Henry Ford.

Therefore, the above proverb by Henry Ford can very well highlight the importance of working together in teams (team-oriented employees). Aswathappa, (2009) in the other hand mentioned some significance of team – oriented employees including;

- Enhances performance
- Cost reduction because of reduced crap, errors and turnover
- Quality decisions

Fourth, flexible and adapting in a meaningful way – For an Organization to be successful, employees should possess the character of flexibility and be willing to pick up new skills and adjust to shifting goals. According to Heathfield, (2018), employees who are flexible normally;

- Reduce negative spillover
- Reduce stress at workplace
- Becomes updated due to adaptation to new situations and ability to learn new things
- Ensure creative and innovative ideas
- Improve self-motivation

More specifically, Mueller, (1992) adds that, managing the employees whoa are flexible is simple and not stressing than those who are not flexible. That is to say, the flexible employees simplify the work of Management in the Organization.

Firth, positive attitude – this is another characteristic of employees that makes an Organization success in its operations. In his work "Organizational Behavior" Aswathappa, (2009) explains that, when the attitude of an employees toward his or her job is positive, there exists job satisfaction. Dissatisfaction exists when the attitude is negative. Job satisfaction often is a collection of attitudes about specific factors of the job.

Gupta, (2011) associates positive attitude with the employees' morale. To make it clear, he indicated the significance of positive attitude among the employees including;

- Higher performance with little supervision
- Low absenteeism
- Low labor turn over
- Good discipline
- Stability and growth of the Organization, therefore, it is necessary for an Organization to have employees with positive attitude.

4

Any Organization would like to have employees with the mentioned qualities; however, it is not easy as it requires careful and appropriate strategies. Recruiting the best employees takes a combination of creativity and diligence. The following are the suggested strategies to be used in obtaining the employees with strong work ethics, self-motivation, team - oriented, flexible and with positive attitude.

First, developing accurate job descriptions before recruitment – the first step is to make sure there is an effective job description for each position in the Organization. Job descriptions should reflect careful thought as to the roles the individual will fill, the skill sets they will need, the personality attributes that are important to completing their tasks, and any relevant experience that would differentiate one applicant from another. Without first preparing job descriptions, many candidate with no quality to the position will apply and will bring unnecessary problems during recruitment process. However, although some applicants will ignore these requirements and respond regardless, including this information will help limiting the number of unqualified applicants.

Second, careful recruitment or hiring – this is the major strategy that can be used to obtain employees with the mentioned qualities. Flippo, (1990) defined the term recruitment as the process of searching for prospective employees. In his work "Human Resource Management", Gupta, (2011), argues that recruitment is the process or a series of activities rather than a single act or event. According to Whitehead, Boschee and Decker (2013), a highly critical aspect of any Principal's job is recruitment and selection of highly quality staff. In education context, the best recruitment of staff is super critical for the success of any school as well as for the Head of school. Recruitment of the right employees therefore, fosters a dynamic of change in the Organization.

For a recruitment process to be successful and obtain employees with the above qualities it requires the following;

- Recruitment policies and procedures need to be clear so as to get the best employees. Whitehead, Boschee and Decker (2013) postulate that, when the recruitment policies are clear, good recruitment and selection yield immense rewards. That is to say, the Organization needs to be clear about the most skills and attributes needed by the

5

applicant through their stipulated policies. According to Martin, (2016) a recruitment policy lays down the organization's objectives for recruitment and the framework to be used to implement the recruitment program. Part of the policy includes coming up with a system to be used to implement the procedures and the programs by selecting the most qualified candidates. A good recruitment policy should provide the following;

i. Its main focus should be to hire candidates whose skills and experiences exceeds the set requirement

ii. Should be unbiased

iii. Help employees to realize their full potential

iv. An equal opportunity for all employees and ensure that every candidate is treated with respect and dignity

v. Transparency, be a merit based and task oriented type of selection

vi. It should abide by the relevant public legislation and policies on employment and hiring relationships

vii. An avenue to integrate the needs of the employee with those of the organization

- Recruitment should follow the following steps as proposed by Whitehead, Boschee and Decker (2013) and Gupta, (2011);
  i. Preliminary screening of credentials
  ii. Screening of credentials
  iii. Reference checks
  iv. In – depth interview
  v. Hiring decision

However, making good selection of employees does not have to be linear. Because hiring the bright and the best candidates alone may not make sense in all circumstances. The skills and ability need to be highly considered in a particular job requirement and market orientation. During the process of recruitment or selection, employers need to avoid any bias so as to get the right applicant.

Third, consideration of past candidates - often when hiring for a position, there are a few talented candidates that end up not making the cut due to timing or other external factors. When recruiting for a similar position, consider re-visiting the resumes of past applicants. These candidates are already familiar with the Organization and may have picked up new skills and experience since the last meeting. When it comes to finding and hiring great employees, employers have to be persistent and willing to think outside the box (Whitehead, Boschee and Decker, 2013: Martin, 2016).

Fourth, including peers in the interview process - Sometimes the best person to interview a candidate is someone already working in the same or similar role rather than the Organization's management team alone. This employee already knows what it takes to excel in the position, and can verify whether candidates have the skills and experience needed to do the job well. Also, current employees can give an accurate description of day-to-day experiences and help candidates better understand what they can expect if hired (Gupta, 2011).

In conclusion, by using these recruitment strategies, it is easy to quickly discover highly qualified, passionate professionals ready to join the Organization team. However, after recruiting the required candidates, retention of the employees should be one of the top priorities. Employee's retention can be done through;

- Fairness and equitable treatment to all employees despite of their differences such as gender, race, religion, tribe, disability and a like.
- Employees should be allowed to use their talents and skills
- There should be a platform for employees to speak their mind freely within the organization
- Provision of training
- Ensuring employment security
- Motivation
- Reduction of status differences within the organization
- Sharing information and
- Recognizing and rewarding good work and creating a free from stress environment in general.

QUESTION TWO

Human Resource Management in its simplest definition means management of organization's manpower or workforce or human resources (Gupta, 2011). Human Resource Management is also defined as a strategic and coherent approach to the management of an organization's most valued assets (the people) working there who individually and collectively contribute to the achievement of its objectives. From this definition, the human resource management is designed to maximize employee performance (Armstrong, 2006). Human resource departments in organizations are typically responsible for a number of activities including; employees' recruitment, training and development, performance appraisal, and rewarding such as managing pay and benefit systems.

The term evolution refers to the gradual change or development of something. Human resource management has gone some changes (evolution) overtime. According to Surbihi (2015), over the past century, there has been an evolution in the concept of "human resources" a term that was not actually used in its current form until the end of the 19th Century. The changes in the culture, politics, and economics of society have influenced these shifts over time.

Welfare Stage (1900–1940s)

During these period personnel functions were performed by supervisors, line managers and early specialists (e.g. recruitment officers, trainers, welfare officers). The early management theorists contributed ideas that would later be incorporated into personnel management theory and practice. Through job design, structured reward systems, 'scientific' selection techniques espoused by scientific management such as Frederick Taylor, Frank Gilbreth and Alfred Sloan. Personnel management practices were refined especially in the recruitment and placement of skilled employees. Behavioral science (or industrial psychology) added psychological testing and motivational systems by Elton Mayo, while management science contributed to performance management programs (Baird, McGrath-Champ, & Kaye, (1999). Personnel functions during this period were mainly restricted to administrative areas (e.g. wage/salary records, minor disciplinary procedures and employee welfare activities).

Key concept used: Labor Management

How they viewed workers: Workers were viewed as tool. Here the behavior of the worker can be manipulated as per the core competencies of the organization and are replaced when they are worn-out.

Welfare and administration (Personnel) Stage (1940s–mid-1970s)

This second stage marks the beginning of a specialist and more professional approach to personnel management. Increased provision of welfare services for employees was seen by some employers as a means of attracting and maintaining employees and ensuring their continued productivity. The Commonwealth Department of Labor and National Service established an Industrial Welfare Division in the 1940s to promote the welfare function, offering emergency training courses to equip practitioners with the necessary skills. These activities were supported by the new human relations theories. In addition, scientific management, the quantitative school and behavioral science contributed employee and management assessment and development techniques such as productivity measures, management planning and control mechanisms such as Drucker, McGregor, Chandler also psychological testing and applications of the emerging employee motivation theories such as Maslow, Hertzberg, McGregor). Many more organizations began to employ specialists to conduct recruitment, training and welfare activities, taking these functions away from line managers (Collings & G. Wood, 2009).

Key concept used: Personnel management

How they viewed workers: Workers were viewed as tool. Here the behavior of the worker can be manipulated as per the core competencies of the organization and are replaced when they are worn-out.

Human Resource Management (Mid-1970s–late 1990s)

During this period the human relations element started to appear to replace welfare and personnel management (Scientific/ conservative methods of managing people). Personnel management was becoming human resource management, representing a change towards the integration of personnel functions, strategically focused on overall organizational effectiveness. Elton Mayo contributed to the establishment of Human Resource Management which used more human approaches. The establishment of the new approaches (HRM) increased productivity and satisfaction among workers (Surbihi, 2015).

Key concept used: Human Resource Management

How they viewed workers: Consider employees as the valuable assets to the organization. It promotes mutuality in terms of goals, responsibility, reward etc.

NB: The roots of human resource management lie in industrial revolution. The prime objective was to have economic gain through labor intensive production of goods. Taylorism- scientific management to increase the efficiency of production of manufacturing goods was widely accepted. The factory system replaced the individual centered traditional system. The workers were merely treated as "cogs in the machine". At this time there was need for establishing a link between the collective representation of labors (unions) and the organization. This link was established as **welfare management** to improve the working conditions and health of workers.

Later, factory system such as assembly line came into existence. Thousands of people worked under single roof. This lead to the need of employing more skilled workers. **Personnel management** mainly involved recruiting people by filling the gaps in the organization, salary payment and supervising them. The Human element was not given importance. As the number of workers increased exponentially, the disputes between them and the organization grew. Workers formed groups called trade unions and wanted their collective voice to be heard. The need for settling the disputes, involving the unions in decision making and fostering healthy work environment lead to **industrial relations.**

Nevertheless, it was discovered that not just economic gains, but also the psychological factors of workers such as motivation levels, healthy working conditions and supervision contribute the efficiency of production. And as the new technologies developed, it necessitated training and development of skills of workers. Performance appraisals needed to be addressed to increase the motivation leveled. As a consequence of this, **Human Resource Management** was born. Human resource development is the new word that aims to bring out not just the existing skills but also the hidden potential of the employee. Human capital management is narrowly synonymous to human resource management in a way that the humans are assumed to be capital, whose knowledge and skills contribute to the development of organization.

10

Strategic human resource management is the new field under human resource management which links human resources to the long term organizational goals. This provides solutions the obstacles related to human resources and fosters competitive advantage for the organization in the long run (Goudar, 2018).

Therefore, the evolution of Human Resource Management can also be categorized into the period before industrial revolution, the period of industrial revolution and the period after industrial period as summarized in the figure below.

Figure 1: shows the evolution of HRM from pre-industrial to post- industrial era

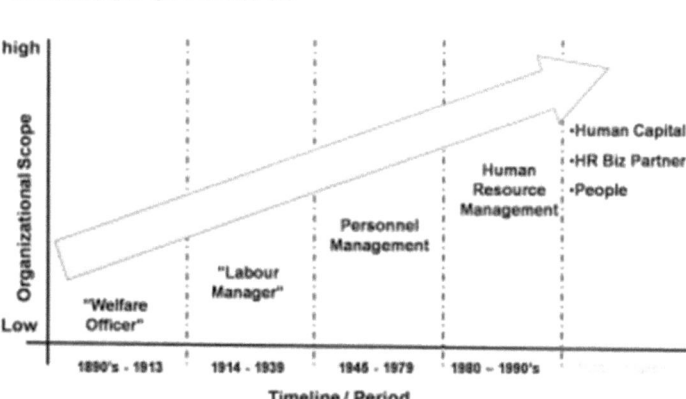

Source: Adopted from Collings & G. Wood, (2009)

Table 1 below shows the differences in various aspects before Human Resource Management and during the Human resource management respectively.

Basis for Comparison	Before HRM	During HRM
Meaning	Concerned with the work force and their relationship with the entity is known as Personnel Management.	The branch of management that focuses on the most effective use of the manpower of an entity, to achieve the organizational goals is known as Human Resource Management.
Approach	Traditional	Modern
Treatment of manpower	Machines or Tools with serious supervision	Asset
Type of function	Routine function	Strategic function
Basis of Pay	Job Evaluation	Performance Evaluation
Management Role	Transactional	Transformational
Communication	Indirect	Direct
Labor Management	Collective Bargaining Contracts	Individual Contracts
Initiatives	Piecemeal	Integrated
Management Actions	Procedure	Business needs
Decision Making	Slow	Fast
Job Design	Division of Labor	Groups/Teams
Focus	Primarily on mundane activities like employee hiring, remunerating, training, and harmony.	Treat manpower of the organization as valued assets, to be valued, used and preserved.

Source: Own construct

In conclusion, the current and future Human Resource Management focuses on; strategic career development. Career development is a huge opportunity for employers because it makes workers perform well their duties and is useful for retention. Transparency is another focus because human beings need transparency, as it allows people to trust the communities and organizations they are affiliate with. Smart Organizations normally peel back the curtains to keep people aligned and motivated toward a common goal. Therefore, the current and future of human resource management perceive employees as valuable assets to the organization.

QUESTION THREE

Austin, (2018) defined employees' management as one way to help turn an underperforming employee around or prevent high-performing employees from becoming a weak performer. The concept of employee management is more than just making sure that people are doing their jobs; it is a variety of procedures and strategies that can help the employer to measure, monitor, and interact with the workforce that plays a huge role in the Organization. Employee management is not just a one-person job. It can comprise of many parts that can take up plenty of time and effort, such as performance reviews, setting up a grievance system, and more.

Wormley (2016) in the other hand postulates that, managing employees involves a few core principles such as;

- Selection - this is about choosing the right employees during the hiring process.
- Measurement - this is about determining how well an employee is performing or meeting goals.
- Monitoring - this is how the employer perform the measurement of employee performance.
- Interaction - this is the daily way an employer and his/her team communicate and work with each other.
- Reward - this is the result of excellent employee performance.
- Discipline - his is the result of lackluster employee performance, and may involve firing

According to URT (2016), Government employee's management in Tanzania is under the President's Office, Public Service Management and Good Governance with the objective of controlling and ensuring integrity in payroll management, budget approval and expenditure; and allocation of staff and institute accountability of human resources management in the Public Service. The following are the main functions of Government employee's management organ in Tanzania;

- To spearhead the implementation of Human Capital Management Information Systems in payroll and all human resources matters in the public service;
- To determine and issue employment permits for new vacancies and replacements for all Public Institutions
- To scrutinize and oversee preparation and implementation of employment rationalization and Personnel Emoluments (PE) Budget for effective Human Capital Management
- To advise on the issues related to implementation of human resource management policies in the Public Service; and
- To coordinate employment rationalization for all Public Institutions

Government employees in school in Tanzania are teachers both in Primary and Secondary schools. Major issues related to the management of these government employees (teachers) in Tanzania can be categorized into three namely; Recruitment and deployment, in-service management and Retirements.

First, recruitment and deployment - teachers are civil servants (government employees) and their recruitment is guided by the public service Act of Employment, Issue No.2 of September 2008. In Tanzania the majority of teachers in Primary and Secondary Schools are employed under permanent and pensionable status, and are entitled to official written contracts undersigned by the Teachers' Service Commission. District councils are their direct employers. According to TESA (2005), the responsibility for the recruitment and deployment of teachers in schools is shared among different state entities;

- The President's Office for Public Service Management is mainly responsible for the formulation of public service polices, the control of the wage bill, staff audits and the issue of guidelines regarding the terms and conditions of service and payments.
- The Ministry of Education Science and Technology has a role to train enough qualified teachers to meet the demand of schools and to monitor the adequacy of teachers' numbers and qualifications.

14

- The Prime Minister's Office for Regional Administration and Local Government is responsible for the coordination of teachers' recruitment and their deployment across local government authorities.
- Local government authorities are in charge of the recruitment and deployment of teachers for primary schools under their jurisdiction. However, primary school teachers from Teachers Training Colleges (TTCs) are normally recruited and deployed by the Permanent Secretary of the Ministry of Education Science and Technology, while the recruitment of teachers for nongovernmental primary schools is processed directly at school level through newspapers and social media advertisements.
- The Ministry of Finance and Economic Affairs is in charge of disbursing all payments including the salaries of teachers (URT, 2016).

The allocation of teachers is taken into account teacher qualification and staffing needs, as determined by the school's capacity. The administration of the teacher supply process follows these steps;

- Ministry of Education Science and Technology issues circulars and guidelines to local government Authorities regarding the deployment of teachers in public schools.
- From the criteria above, the school management estimates the teacher requirement and submits a request to the council director.
- The council consolidates all school requirements and submits them to the Prime Minister's Office for Regional Administration and Local Government
- The Prime Minister's Office for Regional Administration and Local Government submits the national demands to the Ministry of Education Science and Technology for the training of new teachers.
- Then the Prime Minister's Office for Regional Administration and Local Government and the Ministry of Education Science and Technology seek the financial authorization to recruit from the President's Office for Public Service Management
- The President's Office for Public Service Management grants financial authorization. However the number of teachers approved is often lower than the actual requests, because of financial resource constraints in developing countries like Tanzania.

15

After all the above process, teachers are distributed in government schools and the Local Government Authorities proceed to place the teachers in schools. However, factors such as marriage ties, family problems, health conditions and physical disabilities sometimes hinder the effective, efficient and equitable allocation of teachers among schools (TESA, 2005).

The issues of teachers' transfers are managed at the local level, by district councils. When the issue is of public interest, transfers within a council can be decided by the council director, for transfers to other councils within the same region, a permit must be issued by the Regional Administrative Secretary; transfers to other regions only proceed once a permit is granted by the Permanent Secretary of the Prime Minister's Office for Regional Administration and Local Government. When transfers are determined by the authorities on the basis of teacher supply and demand, public service regulations stipulate that teachers receive disturbance and subsistence allowances.

Recruitment of non-teaching and administrative staff in government schools is carried out according to public service regulations and guidelines. The number of such staff depends on the type of school and its size; boarding schools require more nonteaching staff than day schools. The school head is in charge of all administrative functions and activities within the school.

Second, in-service employees management – The management of government employees is done by the President's Office, Public Service Management and Good Governance, however, the Teachers Service Commission (TSC) is the main organ dealing with teachers during their service. The organ was purposely established to do the following; to advice the Minister of education on the maintenance, administration of the service and to strive to secure good conditions of service to all teachers as would from time to time be provided in service regulations, to be a reconciliation organ between the teacher, employer, and trade unions, to maintain a register of all teachers who are in the service, to maintain a record of every teacher in the service, to maintain a system of direct communication with Regional committee on all or any matter relating to the development of teachers service and to ensure that the employer and those committees are performing their functions in accordance with the teachers service regulations (URT, 1989:URT, 2005).

Teachers Service Commission (TSC) therefore, is a vital tool to promote and transfer teachers, exercise disciplinary control over teachers, terminate the employment for teachers and review the demand for and supply of teachers. The issue of termination for example is generally managed at the school and district levels. The process is started by school head teachers who report the matter to the district council, who in turn reports to the Teachers Service Commission, via the district education officer. The Teachers Service Commission investigates, and derives cases to regional and central authorities for corrective measures to be taken (URT, 2005).

- Training of in-service teachers is one of major issues in management of government employees in school. According to Mosha (2006), there is an agreement among scholars about the importance of the teacher and her/his competence in the teaching-learning process. The teacher is the heart of classroom instruction. The effectiveness of the teacher depends on her competence (academically and pedagogically) and efficiency, (ability, work load, and commitment), teaching and learning resources and methods; support from education managers and supervisors (Mosha 2004).

Training the in-service teachers provides opportunities for teachers to explore new roles, develop new instructional techniques, refine their practice and broaden themselves both as educators and as individuals. In Tanzania the Ministry of Education, Science and Technology is responsible for providing policy and financial support for Teacher Professional Development (training) Universities and Teacher Education colleges are responsible for providing training and conducting policy oriented research and providing relevant literature and materials to support teachers in schools.

School management on its part provides support to the teacher on a daily basis through advice, supervision, monitoring and evaluation of the teaching and learning activities. Despite of all those plans, still the training of in-service teachers in Tanzania is not effectively done due to insufficient budget in Educational sector. (Komba & Nkumbi, 2008).

> A study in Guinea shows that teachers who benefited from short but focused professional training (in-service) were more effective than their peers who had benefited from three years of pre-service training (PASEC, 2006).

Therefore, training the in-service government employees in schools is one of the major issues that should not be ignored.

- Motivation for government employees in schools is another important issue in the government employees' management in schools. Teacher motivation becomes a critical factor. On one level, teacher motivation is related to a long list of variables, including whether or not an enabling environment exists and whether or not teachers are equipped to carry out their roles. However, at a basic level, teacher motivation is linked to how teachers feel they are being treated and to the way they perceive their own working and living conditions. For example, if a teacher feels that he or she is being asked to teach too many periods per week, the problem needs to be addressed, regardless of whether or not others in the education system perceive the teacher's workload is too high. The near total absence of issues related to teacher motivation within government documents is evidence of the administration's lack of concern. Though Tanzania's Education and Training Policy of 1995 did have a separate section entitled the "Service and Working Conditions of Teachers," which discussed the importance of teachers' job satisfaction, irregular salary payments for teachers, lack of proper housing for teachers, the low status accorded to teachers, inadequate teaching facilities, and the need to enhance the professional and individual welfare of teachers, its successor, the Primary Education Development Program (PEDP) a more influential government document, made almost no reference to these issues (HAKIELIMU, 2010). Therefore, the issue public teacher's motivation in Tanzania is not taken seriously.

Third, retirement of government employees in schools - Retirement is not a pleasant word for most of employees worldwide, most employees view retirement period as the most dreaded time of their life. The fear of facing the future after retirement "creates an ambiance of disturb' among employees' Retirement is seen by workers as a transition that could lead to psychological, physiological and economic problems (Zonga, 2013). In United republic of Tanzanian law, Sect 17(1) Voluntary age is fifty five while compulsory retirement age by law, sect 17(2) is 60 years and therefore time to retirement is measured in years an employee left to reach the retirement age of 60 years.

Retirement does not occur suddenly in one's working life; rather it involves a series of steps to be taken by the individual during the active working years when he/she was young. In Tanzania the government employees in schools (teachers) face some challenges during their retirement including;

- Small amount of pension given
- Miscalculations of the pension especially when a teachers was upgraded without salary adjustments
- Delay of pension from the date of retirement
- No retirement counseling for the teachers who expect to retire – this is very important because it involve providing prospective retirees with factual information needed to make a pleasant transition from world of work into the world of less rigorous occupational schedules retirement. The concept includes a review of all insurance policies, management of personal income during retirement, explanation of the retirement process, general information about social security, Medicare coverage and acquisition of life skills needed for optional adjustment to retirement roles (Aggrey & Wilson, 2012).

In conclusion, management of government employees in schools in Tanzania comprises of various units including; President's Office, Public Service Management and Good Governance, The Ministry of Education Science and Technology, The Prime Minister's Office for Regional Administration and Local Government, Local government authorities and the Head of Schools respectively. Management of government employees in schools in Tanzania faces various challenges such as poor Human resource policies, deficit of budgets and political issues.

REFERENCE

Aggrey, E. and Wilson, K. (2012). Retirement Planning and Counseling: Issues and Challenges for Teachers in Public Schools in the Sekondi Circuit. *US-China Education Review* A 8 (2012) 755-767

Armstrong, M. (2006). *A Handbook of Human Resource Management Practice*, (10th Ed.).London: Kogan Page.

Aswathappa, K. (2009). *Organizational Behavior* (8th Ed). Mumbai: Himalaya Publishing House.

Austin, T. (2018). *Employment Management.* Retrieved from https://www.groupmgmt.com/blog/post/2018/04/02/What-is-Employee-Management.aspx

Baird, M. and McGrath-Champ, S. in Kaye, L. (1999). Strategic Human Resource Management in Australia: The Human Cost. *International Journal of Manpower*, 20(8), pp. 577–81

Collings & G. Wood (2009). *Human resource management: A critical approach* (pp. 1-16). London: Routledge.

Goudar, M. (2018). *Welfare management, Personnel management, Industrial relations, Human resource management.* Retrieved from https://www.quora.com/What-is-difference-between-welfare-management-personnel-management-industrial-relations-human-resource-management-human-resource-development-human-capital-management-strategic-human-resource-management.

Gupta, C.B. (2011). *Human Resource Management* (13th Ed). New Delhi: Sultan Chand & Sons.

HAKIELIMU, (2010). *The Pivotal Role of Teacher Motivation in Tanzania.* Retrieved from http://hakielimu.org/files/publications/document100pivotal_role_teacher_motivation_en.pdf.

Hanson, E.M. (2003). *Educational Administration and Organizational Behavior* (5th Ed). Boston: Pearson Education, Inc.

Heathfield, S.M. (2018). *What, exactly, is an Employee in Human Resource?* Retrieved from https://www.thebalancecareers.com/what-is-an-employee-1918111.

Komba, W. & Nkumbi, E. (2008). Teacher Professional Development in Tanzania: Perceptions and Practices. *Journal of International Cooperation in Education,* Vol.11 No.3 (2008) pp.67∼ 83.

Martin, J. (2016). *Proven Recruitment Strategies.* Retrieved from https://www.cleverism.com/8-proven-recruitment-strategies/.

Mosha, H. J. (2004). New Direction in Teacher Education for Quality Improvement in Africa. *Papers in Education and Development,* 24, 45-68

Mosha, H. J. (2006). Capacity of school management for Teacher Professional Development inTanzania. Address. *Delivered at a workshop on the Role of universities in promoting basic educationin Tanzania,* held at the Millenium Towers Hotel, Dar es Salaam, Tanzania, May 19.

Mueller, W. S. (1992). *Flexible Working and New Technology: The Psychology of Influence at Work.* Oxford: Blackwell.

Mustafa, G., Glavee-Geo, R., & Rice, P.M. (2017). Teamwork Orientation and Personal Learning: The role of individual cultural values and value congruence. *SA Journal of Industrial Psychology/SA Tydskrif vir Bedryfsielkunde,* 43(0), 1446.

Rafael, A. (1996). What is an Organization? *Who are the Members?* Jerusalem: Hebrew University of Jerusalem.

Reddy, C. (2015). *Ethics in the Workplace.* Retrieved from https://content.wisestep.com/importance-benefits-ethics-workplace.

Surbihi, S. (2015). *Difference Between Personnel Management and Human Resource Management.*Retrived from https://keydifferences.com/difference-between-personnel-management-and-human-resource-management.html.

Tanzania Education Sector Analysis (TESA), (2002). *Primary and Secondary Education Management Issues.* Retrieved from https://poledakar.iiep.unesco.org/sites/default/files/fields/publication_files/chapter7.pdf.

URT (1989). *Teachers Service Commision.* Dar es salaam: Government Printers

URT, (2001). *Primary Education Development Programme.* Dar es Salaam. Retrieved from https://ir.lib.hiroshima-u.ac.jp/files/public/3/34311/20141016201717770074/JICE_11-3_67.pdf.

URT, (2001). *Tanzania Education Status Report.* Dar es Salaam. Retrieved from https://ir.lib.hiroshima-u.ac.jp/files/public/3/34311/20141016201717770074/JICE_11-3_67.pdf.

URT, (2005). *Basic Statistics in Education 1995-2000.* Dar es Salaam. Retrieved from https://ir.lib.hiroshima-u.ac.jp/files/public/3/34311/20141016201717770074/JICE_11-3_67.pdf.

URT, (2016). *Human Capital Management Division. President's Office, Public Service Management and Good Governance.* Retrieved from http://www.utumishi.go.tz/utumishiweb/index.php?option=com_content&view=article&id=13&Itemid=151&lang=en

Wehbe, S. (2017).5 *Important Reasons Why Teamwork Matters.* Retrieved from https://www.potential.com/articles/5-important-reasons-why-teamwork-matters/.

Whitehead, B.M., Boschee, F. & Decker, R.H. (2013). *The Principal: Leadership for a Global Society.*United Kingdom: SAGE Publications, Inc.

Williams, E.A., Duray, R., & Reddy, V. (2006). Teamwork Orientation, group cohesiveness, and Student Learning: A study of the use of teams in online distance education. *Journal of Management Education*, 30(4), 592–616.

Wormley, R. (2016). *Employee Management: The Tools, Tips, and Processes You Need to Build a Better Team in 2016.* Retrieved from https://wheniwork.com/blog/employee-management/

Zonga, S.H.B. (2013). *An Investigation of the Local Government Employees' Attitude towards Retirement.* Master's Thesis, The Open University of Tanzania.